THE TOTALLED ROADKILL COOKBOOK

By B.R. "Buck" Peterson

Illustrations by
J. Angus "Sourdough" McLean

Celestial Arts
Berkeley, California

Printed in Singapore

Cover illustration and design: J. Angus "Sourdough" McLean
Interior design and typesetting: Form Follows Function
Interior illustrations: J. Angus "Sourdough" McLean

Library of Congress Cataloging-in-Publication Data

on file with the publisher

Celestial Arts Publishing
P.O. Box 7123
Berkeley, CA 94707

Other cookbooks in this series:
Come on! Do you really need another cookbook in your kitchen or glove compartment besides this one? Does the phrase "conspicuous consumption" mean anything?

CONTENTS

LUNCH ENTREES

> *"The Great Ones eat up the little ones."*
> PERICLES, PRINCE OF THE RADIAL TYRE

Roadkill as a food source has long and flavorful roots. Experts date initial interest with the invention of the wheel; it wasn't until wheeled vehicles became larger than most of the tastier animals that this method of food-gathering became popular. The early Romans were among the first to shop with wheeled carts and the practice of running over displaced subjects reached its earliest peak with Charleton Heston in *Ben Hur*.

In the United States, the opening and settling of the West sparked a significant breakthrough in the discovery of new foodstuffs. The wagon trains and transcontinental railroads carried the hungry pilgrims to the doorsteps of exotic western fauna; those animals and birds that refused to be domesticated were pushed from their traditional homes into the glare of commuter headlights.

The food selections for the roadside shopper are still richly varied and the supermarkets are open 24

hours. To help the novice, Buck has included with each recipe a likely location symbol—city, suburb, small town, the country, or
the wild—and a symbol for the appropriate
shopping cart to use, whether you're cruising
Wall Street in your limo for capitalist running
dogs or chasing wascally wabbits down Main Street
in the family sedan.

Many of the described foodstuffs may be unfamil-
iar, but what is foreign to one is home cooking to oth-
ers. Even carnivores like us are included. In 1942,
M.F.K. Fisher wrote a book titled *How to Cook a Wolf*,
full of well-thought advice for homemakers during the
rationing of the Big War. As a new war against hunger
looms large, this recipe book continues in that spirit of
public service, lobbying for a national Meals Under
Wheels program.

Roadkill as a food source is the ultimate act of
recycling and a celebration in the studded Wheel of
Fortune. Bone Appetit!

All things Bright and Beautiful
All creatures great and small
With any luck and a gassed-up truck
We're going to take them all.

Key to Symbols

 Taxi

 Limo

 Sports Utility Vehicle

 Family Sedan

 Tractor

 Pickup Truck

 The City

 The Suburbs

 The Small Town

 The Country

 The Wild

*Rumpledkiltskins
Scrapple*

SCRAPES AND SCRAPS

RUMPLEDKILTSKINS

It's No Skin Off My Back

Scraped from the pavement with fur or feathers removed, the rumpled skin of a kilt animal or bird is a popular between-meal snack. This golden treat is worth a king's ransom and guaranteed to put you on the throne.

For the Four-Footed

Preheat oven to 225 degrees. Clean 1 animal skin and cut into squares, scoring fat side into diamonds. Place fat side down in a baking pan covered with lard. Bake for 4 hours, then increase heat to 325 degrees until the cracklins turn golden brown. Remove from oven and drain and salt, or dip in a sauce piquanté. Serves 2 as a meal or 10 as a snack.

For the Birds

Pluck, clean, and remove 1 bird skin (preferably from an upland game bird or fat, grain-fed mallard). Cut skin into strips. In a heated skillet, sauté strips in bacon fat until crisp and brown. Remove and drain. Serves 1 nicely.

SCRAPPLE

The Bored Game

No matter how you play, any combination of pieces is a major score!

Remove eyes and tongue from 1 large animal head (other spare parts can also be used, just clean them reasonably well). In a large soup pot, heat 4 quarts of water and boil head until meat falls off. Remove meat, chop fine, and set aside one pound. Season and strain stock. In a double boiler, bring 4 cups of the strained stock to boil. Add 1 cup corn meal, lower heat, and cook until medium thick. Add reserved meat, 1 sliced onion, 1 teaspoon crushed red pepper, 1 teaspoon black pepper, and 1 teaspoon salt. Cook for 1 hour, then transfer to a greased baking pan. Let cool and cut into slices. In a heated skillet, fry slices in bacon fat. Drain and serve hotdamn for breakfast! Serves the winner and loser and make everyone else offal hungry.

Slurry with a Tinge on Top
Creamed Turtle in its Halved Shell
Piccadillo
Queasydillo
Gravelax
Bumpty Dumpty
Perky Jerky
Squiche Lorraine
Oysters Rocked From a Fella
Tar Tartare

SMACK
TIME

SLURRY WITH A TINGE ON TOP

'Skeets and Bees
and Beetles in a Hurry

*These of them ye may eat; the locust after his kind,
and the bald locust after his kind, and the beetle after
his kind, and the grasshopper after his kind.*
—LEVITICUS 11:22

*The protein-rich stew stirred by your windshield wipers
on a warm, rainy summer night can be enriched by
grasshoppers, beetles, crickets, and honey bees from
your radiator screen. Let creativity be your guide: serve
it chilled as an ishy-ssoise or warmed on your manifold.*

Scrape up 1 cup of bugs. Remove insect wings, wing covers, legs, and heads. In a saucepan, bring 2 cups of salted water to a boil, add cleaned bugs, and cook for 10 minutes. Add 1 stalk chopped celery, 1 diced carrot, 1 diced onion, 1 teaspoon apple cider vinegar, ½ teaspoon sage, 1 tablespoon butter, and salt and pepper to taste. Reduce heat to simmer, cover, and cook until vegetables are tender. Serves 2 hurrying through a food binge.

CREAMED TURTLE IN THE HALVED SHELL

Comes in Its Own Serving Dish

Large snappers will crawl from their warm sandy nesting sites and try to cross a busy country road to the relative safety of a nearby creek. With a little help from Henry Ford and his kin, the tortoise can lose by a hair.

Shuck and clean 2 pounds of turtle meat and cut into 1-inch pieces. In a preheated skillet, melt 3 tablespoons butter and brown meat. Remove meat and set aside. Add 1 large sliced onion, 2 stalks chopped celery, 1 cup cooked lima beans, and enough water to cover. Let simmer for 30 minutes. Add curdled turtle, 3 diced carrots, 3 diced potatoes, 1 small can of tomatoes, and ¼ cup chopped parsley. Salt and pepper to taste, then set aside.

In another skillet, melt 2 cups butter. Stir in 2 cups flour and cook over low heat for several minutes or until golden brown. Slowly whisk in 1 cup cream and cook for 3 to 5 minutes over low heat or until thick. Salt and pepper to taste, then set aside.

Preheat oven to 300 degrees. In a Dutch oven, combine meat mixture and ½ of the creamed sauce and cook for about 45 minutes. Add rest of sauce and heat thoroughly. Serve in cleaned carapace (upper shell) to 4. Myrtle will have to loosen her girdle for this turtle.

PICCADILLO

The Pick of the Litter

When surprised, the nine-banded Dasypus
novemcinctus *or armadillo voluntarily jumps
into harm's way, a reaction that was especially
appreciated during the Great Depression by Okies
fleeing the dust bowl. These "Hoover Hogs" have
since become the official state mascot of Texas and are
now most commonly called "dillos." Nicknames can be
tricky, so remember: a peccadillo is not a peck or quar-
ter-bushel of "dillos," nor is a sarsaparilla a young
female ingrate. For the roadside shopper, the first pick
of the ditch dillos makes a smashing highway hash.*

Clean, slice, and dice 1½ pounds dillo meat. In a preheated skillet, add 1 tablespoon olive oil and sauté
1 chopped onion, ½ chopped green bell pepper, and
1 minced clove garlic until soft. Add dillo meat, 1½ cups
canned tomatoes, 1 tablespoon raisins, 1 teaspoon

capers, 1 tablespoon toasted almonds, 1 chopped and seeded jalapeño pepper, ¼ teaspoon cinnamon, ¼ teaspoon salt, and ¼ teaspoon black pepper. Cook at medium heat and stir until mix is almost dry. Remove from heat and pour mixture over cooked rice. Garnish with 1 chopped cooked egg white and serve with an aside of black beans. Serves 2 picky eaters.

QUEASYDILLOS

Flip, Flop,
and Fry

These easy-to-make turnovers are an essential
part of any dillo-tant's ball.

Clean, dice, and cook 1 pound dillo parts. That wasn't hard, was it? In a preheated skillet, add 1 tablespoon olive oil and sauté 1 chopped onion until soft. Add dillo meat, 1 cooked and diced potato, and 3 slices seeded and chopped jalapeño pepper. Remove from heat, then set aside.

In a mixing bowl, combine 2 cups finely ground dried corn meal (masa harina), 2 tablespoons all purpose flour, ½ teaspoon baking powder, and 1 pinch salt. Sift if you must. In another bowl, combine 2 tablespoons melted butter, 1 egg, and ½ cup milk. Beat together

well, then pour wet ingredients into flour mixture and mix well. Roll out dough into small tortillas and refrigerate until ready to use.

To assemble queasydillos, place 2 tablespoons filling in center of tortilla, seal edges, and fry in hot lard till golden brown. Drain and serve. Serves 4 to 6 easy.

GRAVELAX

Easily Worth One's Salt

*In the Pacific Northwest, the mighty salmon
rule all the waters. When rivers breech their
banks in the spring, a high-center, four-wheel drive
shopping cart is the preferred fishing gear for this
migrating meal.*

Remove bones and gravel from 1 big salmon and cut
out the best fillet, leaving the skin on. In a small bowl,
combine 3 tablespoons black pepper, 5 tablespoons
sugar, and 3 tablespoons salt. Cut fillet in half and
sprinkle mixture over both halves. Cover bottom of
baking dish with 1 cup dill sprigs and place one portion
skin side down on sprigs. Cover with more dill and place

remaining portion skin side up—flesh on flesh. Cover with plastic wrap. Place weight evenly on fish and refrigerate overnight. Turn over package 2 to 3 times in a 24-hour period (18 hours if you can't wait). When hungry, scrape off dill, and pat fish dry. Carve on the bias into thin strips and serve with a mustard sauce. Gets 4 in the mood.

BUMPTY DUMPTY

Stolen from the Display Case of Mrs. Fabergé

If you bump a bird so hard that an egg pops out and in the great fall, the dumped humpty couldn't be put back together again, don't scramble for another egg—just scramble what you have.

In a mixing bowl, beat 1 AAA approved extra large egg with the strength of one king's man until well mixed. In a skillet, melt 1 tablespoon butter and add eggs. Stir slowly, adding 1 tablespoon cream. Cook until done, then salt and pepper to taste. Serves 1 easy appetite.

PERKY JERKY

The Perfect Snack Food

*This recipe smacks of taste infringement and other
legal difficulties. If the freshly-found ground round
is just too perky, try this recipe for the taste and tex-
ture of asphalt-ripened jerky.*

Preheat oven to 150 degrees. Clean and cut fresh found
street-meat into thin strips. In a mixing bowl, combine
1 tablespoon seasoned salt, 1 tablespoon cayenne pepper,
1 tablespoon black pepper, 1 teaspoon thyme, 1 teaspoon
paprika, 1 teaspoon garlic powder, 1 teaspoon dry mustard, 1 teaspoon allspice, and 1 teaspoon salt. Roll strips
in seasoning mixture and bake for 7 to 8 hours with
oven door ajar. Let cool and serve. Serves everyone, even
the quirky.

SQUICHE LORRAINE

Just the Thought of This Dish Makes Me Squicheé Inside!

The quiche of today only slightly resembles the more traditional "cake" or custard pie. With culinary high spirits, serious road foodies combine the freshest ingredients of the open road in a dish that is not only easy to prepare, but also makes a smashing presentation.

Preheat oven to 375 degrees. In a preheated skillet, add 1 tablespoon of bacon fat and sauté 1 thinly sliced onion until soft. In a mixing bowl combine 4 strips crumbled Perky Jerky, sautéed onions, 1 cup diced Swiss cheese, and ¼ cup grated Parmesan cheese. Spread jerky mixture on bottom of 9-inch pastry shell. In another bowl,

combine 2 cups cream, 4 eggs, ¼ teaspoon grated nutmeg, ¼ teaspoon white pepper, and ½ teaspoon salt. Beat lightly and pour on top of jerky mixture. Bake pie for 40 to 45 minutes or until top is nicely browned. Cut into wedges and serve. Serves 6 guests squished around your table.

OYSTERS ROCKED FROM A FELLA

Nuts! Hot Nuts!
Get 'Em From the Peanut Man!

Long considered a robust man's dish, this road deli-cacy found dangling under large furred fellas from the flatlands or mountains holds a reputation similar to its salt-water cousin. It's thought that a steady diet of the dry land version will grow hair on an eater's chest (which, in our post-feminist age, explains the return of the turtleneck sweater to women's fashion).

The hangdown fry of pigs and steers can be used in recipes calling for the salt water variety. Cleaned testicles of a turkey or a chicken are small enough to be pan-fried. Oysters should, however, only be removed from those individuals who no longer have any use for them. In 17th century Italy, young male singers had their "oysters" removed to preserve the soprano or contralto range of their voices, but even the castrati who went on to prosperous careers still felt pretty sore.

Clean and remove coverings and stuff from 1 pair (2) unattached oysters. Split and cut into ½-inch slices. If senior nuts are used, parboil for ten minutes before slicing. Roll sliced nuts in 1 cup flour seasoned with salt and pepper to taste. In a pr eheated skillet, melt ¼ cup butter and fry slices until golden brown. It's the butter that makes the dish as rich as a Rockefeller! Serves one fella traveller nicely.

TAR TARTARE

A Sauced Tartar Has No Need for a 12-Steppe Program

Tartare, or freshly pummelled red meat, began under the saddles of the Mongolians who needed an easy way to tenderize the scavenged remains of eastern Europe. If you're in the mood for scavenging, remember that dark asphalt holds the sun's heat longer than concrete. The fresher the purchase (and the lighter the road), the less likely your raw appetizer will be pre-cooked.

Divide 1 pound of freshly found ground round in half and shape meat into two wheels. Press and fashion 2 egg yolks as hub caps. Cross 2 anchovy fillets across each hub caps like spinners. Stud tires with ½ cup chopped Bermuda onion. Season to taste with salt and pepper. Serves 2 road warriors.

Kitty a la King
Kitty Fritter
Rats A Roni
Sum Yung Pup
Charred Pei
Lapsed Apso
Ground Ground Hog Hog
Pigeon Phlate
German Shepherd Pie
Legs au Kimbo
Chipped Monk on Toast
Mole Molé
Playing Possum
Bumper Thumper
To the Moon, Raccoon
Ricocheted Rabbit
Pepe Le Stew

LUNCH ENTREES

KITTY A LA KING

A Perfect Way
to Serve Your Inner Cat

The most popular feline in the U.S. is the Persian:
a long haired, short, round, Mediterranean cat.
Though the American Short-hair is the oldest recog-
nized American breed, the popular Siamese is the easi-
est breed to get by the short hairs. If you have a
matched set, disjoint the twin before proceeding.

In a large preheated skillet and melt 3 tablespoons butter. Stir in 3 tablespoons flour and add 1½ cup cream.
When sauce is smooth, bring to boil and add 1½ cup
cooked kitty, without any city gritty, 1-6 ounce can
sliced mushrooms, 1 red seeded and chopped jalapeño
pepper, and ¼ cup chopped pimento. Reduce heat and
add 2 beaten egg yolks. Stir until thicker, add ¼ cup
blanched slivered almonds and 1 tablespoon dry sherry.
Salt and pepper to taste. Pour over rice. Serves a couple
royally.

KITTY FRITTER

A Flat Cat in a Hat is Worth More Than a Puss in a Boot

One of history's most notorious kitties owned the Long Branch Saloon in Dodge City, where exotic felines frittered their time away with many a lonely critter. On many rowdy nights, the saloon was full of misadventure for the hapless. When the gunsmoke finally cleared, a miss'd kitty was often the only one still standing amidst all the litter.

Take 1 almost miss'd kitty and strip joints of edible meat. Clean and mince meat, shape into small balls, and set aside. In a mixing bowl, combine 1⅓ cup flour, 1 tablespoon melted butter, ½ teaspoon salt, and ½ teaspoon black pepper. Add ¾ cup flat or Canadian beer and stir well. Cover and refrigerate 3 to 6 hours. In a deep fat fryer, heat 3 cups cooking oil to 365 degrees. Dip minced kitty meat balls into batter and cook until golden brown. Serves 2 tomcatting-around types.

RATS O' RONI
The Sacramento Treat

Of all the four-legged rats found in large cities,
the uptown rodents—hamsters, white mice, and
guinea pigs—are quite out of reach of the street,
and busy being tortured by Ritalin-crazed young-
sters in high rise apartments. Downtown rats are well
within reach, scurrying about abandoned nightscapes
like urban cowboys. Round 'em up!

In a preheated skillet, heat ¼ cup olive oil. Fry 3 cups
cooked white rice until brown, then add 1 cup chopped
and cooked ratso meat, ½ cup chopped celery, ½ cup
minced scallions, and 1 teaspoon freshly ground pepper.
In a mixing bowl, beat two eggs and stir into meat mixture. Heat thoroughly. You can serve 2 or you can serve
1. But usually there are none.

SUM YUNG PUP

How Much is That Doggie Through the Windshield?

According to ancient Chinese tradition, those who eat dog meat during the hot "dog days" of summer avoid heat prostration. Salt tablets and cool shade will also help.

Whoopie ti-yi-yo, git along little doggies,
It's all your misfortune and none of my own.
Whoopie ti-yi-yo, git along little doggies,
Here in my belly will be your new home.

Skin, clean, debone, and chop 1 yung pup. In a preheated wok, add 2 tablespoons olive oil and sauté 1 tablespoon chopped ginger and 1 clove minced garlic. Wok the dog until browned. Add 1 tablespoon sugar, 1 teaspoon soy sauce, and ½ cup water and stir. Simmer for 20 minutes or until tender. This puppy will serve 1 yuppy.

CHARRED PEI

Throw This Little Shrimp on the Barbie!

There are an estimated 50 million dogs in the United States. With 20 million pounds of dog doo produced daily, chances are you just stepped in some.

The formal dog family is registered into seven major groups and each group has individuals that can and do live most anywhere. Sporting, Working, and Herding dogs are most at home in the country while Terriers, Toys, Non-Sporting, and Hounds fit the smaller urban spaces. Somewhere there's an exotic hound waiting to grace your plate and palate.

Special note to the overly concerned: The Pei has so much loose skin, a small fillet will not be missed.

Preheat broiler or prepare a grill. Remove excess fat from 1 fresh piece of pei and score edges to prevent curling. Grease grill grid and place meat 3 inches from heat source and char top side until brown. Do the other side a good turn. Season to taste and add a dollop of garlic butter. Serve yourself on a pei plate.

LAPSED APSO

A Robust and Daring Use
of an Exotic Foodstuff

*The following is not just another shaggy dog
story: The little Tibetan llaso was originally used to
stand watch in the royal inner chambers while a
mastiff took the front door. When this regal runt ven-
tured outside, the golden opportunity for a massive stiff
to the apso that yaps so would occur.*

Preheat oven to 350 degrees. Clean and skin 1 collapsed apso and rub 1 tablespoon chopped fresh chives, 1 tablespoon thyme, 1 tablespoon dried thyme, and 1 tablespoon black pepper into meat. Place poached pooch in a roasting pan and bake for 30 minutes. Add 1 cup brandy to pan for baste and bake for another 30 minutes or until a hind leg moves to and fro. Make gravy in pan by adding 3 tablespoons all purpose flour and 1 cup cream. Season to taste and stir until thick. Slice up and serve 2 lapsed vegetarians. Howl if more is needed.

GROUND GROUND
HOG HOG

Only the Shadow Knows

The largest small town or suburban rodent is the American marmot. If this amateur meteorologist pokes his head out on a sunny February 2, you will have six more weeks of winter. That alone is a good a reason not to let him see his shadow.

The following recipe begs the question: How many woodchucks can a good Buck shuck if a good Buck could shuck woodchucks?

Prepare a grill. Shuck 1 woodchuck and grind hog meat until you have two pounds, then chuck the rest in the Punxsutawney land-phil. In a large bowl, combine the hog meat with 1 pound sweet Italian sausage, 1 clove minced garlic, 1 teaspoon Worcestershire sauce, and ¼ cup crumbled blue cheese. For this lean meat to hold together, add one beaten egg to each pound of meat mixture and mix well. Form into patties and broil to desired doneness. Serves 2 food hogs.

PIGEON PHLATE

A Bird in the Sand
is Worth Two in the Bush

*In the city, pigeon lovers have the choice of the un-
likely squab—the immature bird that fell, not flew,
out of its nest—or the more available park resident. No
need to squabble. If you decide on an older homer, grab
one near an active park bench. Toed the way they are,
these winged beggars are easy to take and so full of
bread crumbs, you may not need a stuffing mix.*

Preheat oven to 350 degrees. In a saucepan, place 2
phlattened pigeon philets, cover with either vegetable or
chicken broth and cook on medium heat until tender.
Drain and grind the meat to a fine mince. In a mixing
bowl, combine meat with 2 chopped hardboiled eggs
and set aside. In a preheated skillet, heat 2 tablespoons
olive oil and sauté ½ cup chopped onions until soft. To

meat mixture add onions, 1 teaspoon cognac, ½ teaspoon allspice, and salt and pepper to taste and mix well. Pack paste in a buttered mold and bake for 30 minutes or until set. This stuff is so good you'll pigeon hole the remains. Serves you and the cat.

GERMAN SHEPHERD PIE

For Those Late Night Mac (Truck) Attacks

There are at least 101 ways to cook a Dalmatian. Should you find a Lassie under your chassis, any beef recipe will do. This meaty dish is appropriate for the uber-rascal that thins, rather than keeps watch over, his flock by night.

Preheat oven to 350 degrees. Cube 1 pound cooked lean, mean, mongrel machine (preferably any kin of Rin Tin Tin) and set aside. In a preheated skillet, melt 2 tablespoons butter and sauté 1 cup chopped onions, ½ cup chopped carrots, ¼ cup chopped celery, and 2 tablespoons chopped fresh parsley until onions are soft. Sprinkle with 3 tablespoons flour and stir. Add 2 tablespoons tomato paste, ½ cup dry white wine (not the cheap stuff), 1½ cups chicken stock, 1 teaspoon

Worcestershire sauce, and ½ teaspoon black pepper, stirring rapidly. Simmer for 10 minutes and stir in cubed meat and 1 cup cooked corn niblets. Cook five more minutes. In a baking dish, pour meat and sauce and cover with 3 cups mashed potatoes. Sprinkle ½ cup grated cheese in a sprightly fashion on top of the mashed potatoes and bake for 30 to 45 minutes until dish is hot and cheese is melted. Serves 4 growling stomachs.

LEGS AU KIMBO

A Froggie Went a' Courting and He Did Fry, Oh-Oh ...

An attractive, single, valley princess would do well to leave her carriage in the garage on rainy summer nights if she thinks a handsome young prince might be leapfrogging across the slippery roads. Knowing that royalty is nigh impossible to confirm in the dark, smart ladies-in-waiting are out bumper-kissing as many good-eating frogs as possible.

Remove hind legs. Once they stop twitching, remove their feet. Wash, strip skin, and lay in shallow baking dish. Brush 2 tablespoons cognac over top of legs and refrigerate for 2 to 4 hours. Remove and pat dry. In a preheated skillet, melt 1 tablespoon butter and sauté ¼ cup thinly sliced onions and 1 clove minced garlic. Add legs to skillet and fry until golden brown. Four large frogs legs will serve 2 persons. Five large frog legs begs the question: Where's the sixth?

CHIPPED MONK ON TOAST

Epistrophy on Whole Wheat

Shopping in open air markets for little furred animals such as gophers and tree or ground squirrels can be a popular Sunday activity for the whole family. A recreational golfer will be par for the course if a bushy-tail is taken with a chip shot off the golf cart. An extra bonus is awarded to any serious lover of music for chipping any ground rodent that sings, particularly any answering to the name Alvin, Theodore, or Simon.

Skin, clean, debone, and chip 2 6-ounce critters. In a skillet, heat 4 tablespoons butter and sauté 4 tablespoons minced green bell peppers and 3 tablespoons minced onions until soft. Add 4 tablespoons flour, 3 cups milk, chipped meat, and 1 teaspoon grated nutmeg. Simmer until sauce thickens and season with a pinch of dried parsley, a thimble of dry sherry or port, and a dash of paprika. Let Chip and Dale dance on hot toast points. Serves 2 on the 19th hole.

MOLE MOLE

Ain't No Molehill High Enough

The most irksome suburban rodent is the mole, whose underground roadway system has no easy on-ramp. By using a combination of noise and smoke bombs, you can put the prime ingredient of this popular Tex-Mex dish in your headlights. The following recipe also works well with water-dwelling rats. To remove the edible parts of thick-skinned marsh rodents such as muskrats, nutria, and beaver, LEAVE IT TO THE CLEAVER!

In a deep fryer, heat 2 cups olive oil and 3 seeded, chopped jalapeño peppers to 370 degrees. Skin, debone, rinse, and cube 1 pound mole meat. Dip meat in 2 cups nonfat milk (watch that waistline!), then roll in 1 cup seasoned flour, and deepfry for 5 minutes. Drain and place in baking dish with 6 seeded, sliced green bell peppers.

Preheat oven to 225 degrees. In a dry preheated skillet, toast 1½ tablespoons sesame seeds, ½ cup pine nuts, and ¾ cup blanched almonds until brown. Set aside. Grind together 2 corn tortillas and 3 seeded,

chopped jalapeño peppers. Set aside. In a preheated skillet, heat 2 tablespoons olive oil and sauté 3 cloves minced garlic until brown. Add 2 cups peeled tomatoes, 1 teaspoon cinnamon, toasted seeds and nuts, and ground tortillas and peppers. Pour sauce over meat and cook for 3 hours. Add 2 ounces grated unsweetened chocolate just before serving. Serves 2, too, too much.

PLAYING POSSUM

Method Acting at its Tastiest

The American opossum is a silly lil' animal that plays 'possum when in danger, which is mighty confusing when you think about it. These low riders would probably live longer if they played chicken instead. While the 'possum is busy playing itself, remove the insides and outsides. By the time this protein-rich berry eater smells the sweet potatoes, it'll think it died and passed through the 'possum pearly gates. It will have.

Skin, clean, and scrape 1 'possum. Parboil for several hours (patience is a must), then drain and let cool. Preheat oven to 350 degrees. In a small bowl, combine 1 teaspoon salt, 1 teaspoon black pepper, and 1 teaspoon cayenne pepper. Rub seasonings into possum and place

in a baking pan. Cut 4 sweet 'po-taters in half and place around possum. Cover and bake for 1 hour. Remove pan and sprinkle sweet potatoes and possum with 1 cup brown sugar, 1 tablespoon lemon juice, and 2 table-spoons butter. Bake uncovered until surface is browned. This awesome possum serves 4.

BUMPER THUMPER

Hare Today, Gone Tomorrow

Under a commission from the Hallmarke Institute, a lobbying group dedicated to turn every religious holiday into a shopping frenzy, B. Trix Potted wrote a series of stories about a rabbit with attention deficiency disorder. With the velvet gloves of the English tea garden set, she described the insane flippity, floppity world of the bunny trail that marketers spun into a lot of colored eggs for sister Sue, orchids for your mom, and the Easter bonnet, too. Maybe Mr. McGregor's chase of Peter Cottontail was not such a hare-brained idea after all.

In a large pot, boil 1 skinned, cleaned, and properly thumped rabbit for 45 minutes or until tender. Preheat oven to 350 degrees. Remove meat from carcass and finely chop. In a mixing bowl, combine rabbit meat with ½ pound fat pork, ½ clove minced garlic, ¼ teaspoon nutmeg, ¼ teaspoon thyme, ¼ teaspoon black pepper,

and ¼ teaspoon salt. Mix well until it has the consistency of paste. Place mixture in a baking dish, cover, and cook for 2 hours. Just before serving, pour 1 cup melted butter over potted rabbit. Serves 2 needy and greedy eaters.

TO THE MOON, RACCOON

Shine On, Shine On Harvest Coon, Up in the Sky

An old ringtail is one tough customer! Even if the launch or lift-off went as planned, expert ground control is essential for a proper recovery of the spaced craft.

Preheat oven 350 degrees. Skin and clean 1 rocketed raccoon and place in baking pan with 2 peeled, quartered carrots, 2 small onions, and 2 peeled, quartered potatoes. Bake covered for 1 hour. Remove pan and add ½ cup brandy and 1½ cup water and bake uncovered for another hour, using drippings as baste. Season according to season. It'll be the best meal you and 3 of your close personal friends have had in a coon's age.

RICOCHETED RABBIT

Bye-Bye Baby Bunted

*"Thou woldest fynde an hare
under thy radial tyre, ther."*
GEOFFREY CHAUCER

*As all roadside shoppers know, the feet of Benjamin
Bunny should be saved and pickled for good luck. Both
the foot of the hare and the rabbit are prized charms. It
is the fertile nature of both animals that gives its body
parts the association with prosperity. Any part of the
rabbit promises good fortune; for the buck or male
rabbit, the foot appendage is more willingly donated.*

Preheat oven to 350 degrees. Skin, clean, debone, and cut
1 grazed bunny into bite-size pieces. Roll bunny bits in
½ cup seasoned flour. In a baking pan, heat 2 tablespoons olive oil and brown bunny with ½ cup sliced
onions. Add 1 cup chicken stock and bake covered for
1½ hours. Remove pan and stir in 2 tablespoons flour
to make gravy. Serves 2 of the less strict hare krishnas.

PEPE LE STEW

Phew! Was That You?

The word "skunk" comes from the Algonquin word "squncke," meaning "he who squirts." By direct experience, "squncke" was soon understood by New World explorers. It wasn't until tomato juice was commercially available that relief from le phew became an olfactory nerve away. These lil' stinkers have since become pets and middle-of-the-road cartoon characters.

This American representative of the polecat family has the best natural black fur for long wear and good looks; the preferred donors for winter pelts are the northern "squnckes." Caution is recommended while appropriating jacket material from these odor-able critters.

Preheat oven to 350 degrees. Skin, clean, debone, and cut 1 de-"flower"-ed skunk into bite-size pieces. In baking pan or Dutch oven, melt ½ cup butter and brown meat with 1 large chopped onion. Add 2 cups chopped tomatoes, 1 cup white wine, and enough water to cover. Cover and simmer for approximately one hour or until meat is tender. Remove pan and add 2 peeled, quartered potatoes, 3 sliced carrots, and 4 chopped celery stalks. Bake uncovered for 45 minutes or until tender. Serves a phew.

Croq Au Vin
Mou Shu Moo
Horned Beef Hash
Blackened Blue Stallion
Wrack of Lamb
Lamb Chops in a Shari Sauce
Mixed Grill
Smoked Smokey
Minced Meat Pie
Carnage Asada
Totallini Assortini
Mustang Sully
En Route En Crouté

DINNER ENTREES

CROQ AU VIN

It's a Fowl World
After All

These playful farm birds love to run forthrightly towards your shopping cart, so don't chicken out at the last moment. Cross the fowl line, especially if you have a chance to croq an aspiring bantam of the opera.

Pluck, clean, and quarter 1 croq-ed coq. In a preheated skillet, cook ¼ pound chopped salt pork until crisp. Remove and reserve the fat. Brown chicken in fat, then add 4 chopped onions and 2 cups whole mushrooms. Cover and cook until onions are soft and start to brown. Remove chicken and pour off most of the fat. Sauté 3 chopped shallots and 1 clove minced garlic for 1 minute, then add 2 cups dry red wine, and 1 teaspoon brandy. Stir well and heat until boiling. Replace chicken and add

enough water to cover bird. Add cooked salt pork and simmer until chicken is tender. Remove chicken. Add 2 tablespoons butter, 2 tablespoons flour, 1 tablespoon chopped fresh parsley, ⅛ teaspoon thyme to drippings, simmer until thick, and serve over chicken. Serves 2, no, 4. That's not right. Make it 3. Or just eat it yourself.

MOU SHU MOO

E. Coli Prefers
His Undercooked

"Dairy cows are stupid. They're born stupid, live stupid, and die stupid. I'm amazed that anyone who drinks milk doesn't get stupid as well."

OLD McDONALD, WITH A MOO-MOO HERE
AND A MOO-MOO THERE

Slice 1 pound moo meat into thin 2-inch strips. In a mixing bowl, combine 2 teaspoons soy sauce and 1 teaspoon cornstarch. Marinate the meat strips in this mixture for 1 hour. In a preheated wok, heat 1 tablespoon olive oil and fry 2 beaten eggs on both sides until set hard, remove and cut into strips. *Mou Shou* in Chinese means yellow cassia blossom, symbolized in this dish by the little bits of scrambled eggs. Add moo meat, 4 large thinly sliced mushroom caps, 1 large thinly sliced

reconstituted dried Chinese mushroom, ½ cup thinly sliced bamboo shoots, three tablespoons water, 2 tablespoons soy sauce, ½ teaspoon sugar, and 1 clove minced garlic to wok and cook until meat is medium rare. Add 1 tablespoon water and 1 teaspoon cornstarch to mixture. Cook until it thickens, then adding eggs and 2 chopped green onions, stirring for ½ minute or so. Remove from heat and serve over steamed rice. The moo serves two.

"These twelve-hundred-pound dummies can be taught to go into a stanchion for all day, every day. If they were smart, we'd be in big trouble!"

KRIS, THE MINNESOTA MILK MARM

HORNED BEEF HASH

Locked on the Horns
of a Dilemma

Of all the beef cattle raised for off-road shopping, the Longhorn steer has the most exotic past. Descendants of Spanish cattle brought to the New World by Christopher Columbus, this formerly free-ranging animal is now seen more often in old western movies, where the phrase, "Time to rustle up a little grub," has a double meaning. Toot your own horn if you take one of these high plains drifters!

Grind 2 pounds of rustled up de-horned beef. In a mixing bowl, combine beef with 2 large cooked, diced potatoes, 1 large chopped onion, ½ cup chopped green bell peppers, and 1 beaten egg and mix well. In a preheated skillet, melt 1 tablespoon butter and cook mixture until

hash is hot. Cook until the bottom is crusty and then turn over. Repeat on other side. For an extra hardy hash, form individual patties before cooking and place one egg fried over-easy on each before serving. This grub stakes 4.

BLACKENED BLUE STALLION

A Thorough-Dead Thoroughbred

Horse meat as a food source has a long noble history. In a royal hunger, foodie Richard III shouted, "A horse! A horse! My kingdom for a horse!" As you cruise the backlots with your truck and empty trailer, don't worry if you find yourself in a one-horse town. You may still be able to hit that gift horse in the mouth.

The large horse family includes the donkey (which is really an ass), with males called jackasses and females jennys or jennettes. A burro is a Mexican term for a smaller ass and a large ass comes from eating too many Mexican burritos. Mules are half-ass, a hybrid of a female horse and a male ass, and twenty mules tied together in a team make a marvelous household cleaner.

Prepare a real grill, not charcoal. Take 1 filly fillet and butter it. In a mixing bowl, combine 2 tablespoons paprika, 2 tablespoons salt, 1 tablespoon white pepper, 1 tablespoon cayenne pepper, 1 tablespoon black pepper, 1 tablespoon garlic powder, and 1 tablespoon onion powder and mix well. Press both sides of fillet into mixture of seasonings. Place fillet on grill with a pat of butter on top to flare the heat. Grill two minutes each side. Serve yourself right with a side of horseradish.

WRACK
OF LAMB

Wrack 'Em Up!

*Thomas Edison spoke these four lines, the first
words of recorded human speech, into his invention,
the phonograph on November 24, 1877:*

> Mary had a little lamb,
> Its fleece was white as snow.
> Everywhere that Mary went,
> The lamb was sure to go.

*Due to technical difficulties, the second verse did not
make it:*

> Mary, Mary, quite contrary,
> Where did your little lamb go?
> With heavy vehicular traffic,
> To tasty chops all in a row.

Preheat oven to 400 degrees. Skin and clean 1 whacked rack of young lamb (rib end of saddle loin). Trim excess fat and tissue. Rub rack with 2 tablespoons butter and 1 clove garlic or rub with 2 tablespoons Dijon mustard and roll in seasoned bread crumbs. Roast on a metal rack in a shallow pan for 1 hour or until internal temperature reaches 145 degrees. Carve into chops and serve with roasted garlic and grilled vegetables. Serves 4 roadside shoppers on the lam.

LAMB CHOPS IN A SHARI SAUCE

I'm a Poor Little Hand Puppet Who Has Lost Its Way

There is no need to feel sheepish about this dish. Lamb is a staple food item in most cultures. When properly prepared, a lambasted little woolly wins hands down.

Preheat oven to 350 degrees. Whip and poof 2 lamb chops, one hand high. Brown chops in buttered baking dish, then set aside. In a preheated skillet, melt 2 tablespoons butter and add 2 tablespoons flour. Cook for 1 minute, then add ½ cup extra dry shari, ½ cup poultry or beef stock, and ¼ cup heavy cream. Remove from heat and stir until sauce thickens. Pour sauce over chops, cover and bake for 30 minutes. Serves Shari and her best friend handily.

MIXED GRILL

As Buck Says,
It's All Take-Out Food!

A traditional mixed grill features fowl, sausage, lamb chops, and pork chops, with an accompaniment of garlic potatoes. On the open road, however, what's mixed in your grill is determined by your location, time of day and year, and whether you've been naughty or nice. It's unlikely you will acquire the shy Bullwinkle or the majestic elk, but upland game birds, pronghorn antelope, and the slower-witted mule deer are served up at dusk.

De-feather and de-fur 4 pounds assorted road meats. In a mixing bowl, combine 1 cup soy sauce, ½ cup olive oil, 1 clove minced garlic, ½ teaspoon Worcestershire sauce, ½ teaspoon dry mustard, 1 teaspoon black pepper, and 1 teaspoon salt. Marinate meats for 24 hours. Prepare a grill and grill mixed bag medium rare. Serve with broiled tomatoes and mushrooms wrapped in bacon. Serves 4 of those who care enough to eat the very best.

SMOKED SMOKEY

The Smoking Lamp is Lit

The nation's most famous bear marked his golden anniversary in 1994. Smokey's 50 years in the fire protection business was quietly celebrated with a smoker at the U.S. Park Service headquarters. Guess who got smoked?

Bears just want to be left alone, whether playing on the polar ice cap or raiding a park dump. They are typically solitary animals and become unbearable only when they have a toothache, a butt softened by buckshot, or after a fair-haired girl eats all their porridge. Most shoppers encounter bears only in national parks; if you are interested in rearranging the master Plan of the Care Bear, this recipe from a famous roadside attraction fills the bill.

Investors in a bear market have reason to be wary and treat the bruin as pork; if you bake bear, an internal temperature of 140 degrees avoids trichinosis.

Skin and clean 1 raw 5 pound rump roast. Cure the big bruin butt in a solution made of 5 gallons water, 6 pounds salt, and 3 pounds brown sugar for three weeks. Using an enormous hypodermic syringe, inject ounce of brine in center near bones. Turn butt every 3 to 4 days. When ready, wash and scrub in lukewarm water, then cold water. Smoke with your favorite hardwood at 90 degrees up to 4 days. This yummi bear serves 4 tummies.

MINCED MEAT PIE

A Pie in the Face of Disaster

This traditional old world road dish is appropriate for all the holidays, particularly as a Christmas gift for the in-laws and other less fortunates.

In a large pot, combine 2 pounds freshly minced road meat, ¼ pound chopped beef suet, 5 cups seedless raisins, 4 cups chopped tart apples, 2 cups currants, 3 cups apple cider, 2 cups brown sugar, 1½ cups granulated sugar, ½ cup chopped candied citron, ½ cup cider vinegar, 1 cup chopped nuts, ¼ cup grated orange peel, 1½ teaspoon ground nutmeg, 1 teaspoon ground cloves, 1 teaspoon cinnamon, 1 teaspoon mace, 1 teaspoon salt, 1 teaspoon pepper, and 2 ounces dark rum (1 for the mix, 1 for the cook). Heat until boiling, then reduce heat and cover. Simmer for two hours, stirring occasionally. Let cool. Stir in any remaining rum the cook hasn't gargled.

Preheat oven to 425 degrees. In a 9-inch pie plate, lay out 1 pre-rolled pie crust. Fill with 5 cups minced meat, then cover with another pre-rolled pie crust. Seal edges and cut several slits on top. In a mixing bowl, beat together 1 egg and 1 tablespoon water. Brush top of pie with egg mixture, then bake for 10 minutes. Reduce heat to 350 degrees and bake for another 40 minutes, or until crust is brown. Don't mince around! Slice this monster and serve 4.

CARNAGE ASADA

Don't Be So Namby-Bambi

The larger toasted portions found in curbside carnage often belong to whitetail deer. The whitetail deer has unwisely chosen to live in the eastern hardwoods and brushlands bordering the most populated areas of the country. With Vatican-approved family planning, the whitetail population has exploded, pushing these four-legged yard and garden pests to the front of the highway supermarket. The young and the restless are usually the first (but not the last) blinded by the bright city lights.

Even the Big Bad Wolf knows a serving of venison, especially the spotted variety, has ⅓ fewer calories, twice the protein, and ¼ the fat of an equal portion of trimmed, choice raw beef. Cruise and choose.

Preheat oven to 350 degrees. In a preheated skillet, heat
1 tablespoon olive oil and sauté 1 small chopped onion
until soft. Set aside. Fry 1 breakfast-sized purloined
sirloin cut from Bambi's bum until spots disappear.
Cover slammed Bambi with 4 sliced jalapeño or red bell
peppers, onions, and ½ cup grated Monterey Jack cheese.
Place in 350 degree oven until asada-ed or cheese melts.
Serve to your dearly beloved.

TOTALLINI ASSORTITI

For Things That Get Bumped in the Night

This pasted pasta dish is particularly good for using left-out leftovers. When choosing a wine to serve with this dish, remember: white with fowl, red with beef or beef by-products, and rosé with all bye-bye products.

In a preheated skillet, heat 1 tablespoon olive oil and sauté 3 tablespoons minced fennel bulb until soft. Add 3 tablespoons chopped chives and sauté for 30 seconds. Remove from heat and stir in ½ pound ground, pre-cooked assorted totally totalled road chunks and 1 beaten egg. Salt and pepper to taste and set aside.

In a mixing bowl, combine 3 cups sifted flour and 4 beaten eggs and mix to form a ball. Turn out on a floured surface and knead dough until smooth and stiff. Roll out to ¹⁄₁₆-inch thickness and cut into 2-inch circles. Place 1 tablespoon filling in center of circle and fold

over, wetting edges with water. Wrap half-shell around small finger, touching ends. Drop in boiling water for 10 minutes, then remove and set aside.

In a preheated saucepan, melt 2 tablespoons butter. Add 1½ tablespoons flour and stir until blended, then add 1 cup heavy cream. Pour sauce over totallini and dust with fresh grated Parmesan cheese or toss with proscuitto and fresh cooked peas. Color with pinch of chopped fresh parsley. Serves 1 big or 2 small Italians.

MUSTANG SULLY

A Spaghetti Western

The Spanish explorer, Cortez first introduced horses to North America in the early 1500s. As this stock grew, some ran free and formed feral herds called mesteños. These mustangs have come to symbolize the few remaining vestiges of the Wild West and it takes one four-wheeled, turbo-charged steed to slow the other free spirit down.

In a preheated skillet, heat ½ olive oil and brown ¾ pound ground mustang meat and ¼ pound ground pig meat. Add 1 cup chopped onions and sauté till golden soft. Add 1 clove minced garlic, 2 cups tomatoes, ¼ cup tomato paste, and ½ cup water or bouillon and stir well. Let simmer for ½ hour, then add 1 cup red wine, 1 teaspoon basil, 1 teaspoon salt, and ½ teaspoon black pepper. Cover and let simmer for 2 to 3 hours, adding water as needed. Before serving, stir in 1 cup of Romano cheese and cook until melted. Serve the all dented mustang over al dente noodles to 2 slowpoke cowpokes.

EN ROUTE
EN CROUTE

On the Road Again

On that long lonesome highway, a wide variety of wild animals will vie for your culinary attentions. This all-purpose preparation is specifically designed for a roadside shopper's break-and-bake.

Skin and clean 1 large 2 to 3 pound tenderloin taken en route. In a mixing bowl, combine 4 cups flour, 1 cup shortening, and 1½ teaspoon salt. Make an impression in middle, and fold in 3 eggs one at a time and ½ cup water. Turn out on a floured surface and knead dough until smooth and stiff. Roll into ball, cover, and let sit for 2 to 3 hours in a warm (70 degrees) place. Preheat oven to 300 degrees. Roll out dough about ¼-inch thick and place meat on the dough. In a mixing bowl, beat together 1 egg and 1 tablespoon water. Coat meat with egg wash and fold over croute, sealing seams with egg white. Slash steam vents in dough casing and place on baking sheet. Bake for 2 hours and serve on a platter garnished with whatever looks pretty. Serves 4 louts en doubt.

A Dog Gone Good Meal
Smothered Mother
Cat on a Hot Thin Roof

JUST
DESSERTS

A DOG GONE GOOD MEAL

Hot Diggity, Dog Diggity

*In this age of permissiveness, don't excuse the
actions of an ungrateful cur who likes a piece or
rather taste of your action by saying, "It's only a
dog." Drive noisily by the Lair of the Dog That Bit You
with a bright cloth stuck under a hub cap and you'll put
a permanent part in the Hair of the Dog That Hit You.*

Skin and clean 1 round hound. Remove meat from the
bones and cut into bite-sized pieces, about the same size
as the bite on your leg. (With this recipe, each bite you
take will take a bite out of crime). Season each piece
with salt and pepper and then roll in flour. In a preheated skillet, heat 2 tablespoons olive oil and fry the dog
pieces until brown. Remove pieces and place in a large
crockpot or any slow cooker. Add 3 cans mushroom
soup, 1 cup whole kernel corn, 1 pound of sliced mushrooms, 1 large chopped onion, 1 chopped celery stalk,

¼ teaspoon sugar, and three cups water. Turn crockpot control to high for 30 minutes, then add 3 cups sour cream and turn down to low. Go back to bed for another 8 hours. You've earned it. To really put on the dog, serve over rice with a ½ tablespoon fresh, chopped parsley. Woof this down and remember to clean your plate as you'll have no one to throw the scraps to! Serves 4 growling appetites.

SMOTHERED MOTHER

Who Wouldn't Enjoy a Little Goose Now and Then?

For anyone who has suffered a domestic goose charge in the yard, a wild goose chase in the park, and/or grew up dreaming of ladybird house fires, nine-day-old pease-porridge, and an old woman in a shoe who needed sex counseling, take a gander at the following road recipe.

To properly smother a bird, it's traditional to split the back and weigh the breast down as it cooks in an iron skillet. To properly smother this big bird, use a pillow from one of her dreadful bedtime story-telling sessions. If in the purchase, the good mother falls to pieces, rub each piece in butter, then roll in 1 cup seasoned flour. Preheat oven to 225 degrees. In a preheated skillet, melt 2 tablespoons butter and brown floured goose parts. Transfer goose parts to baking dish. Sauté 1 cup sliced

onions, ½ cup chopped jalapeño peppers, and 1 cup light cream until onions are soft. Pour mixture over goose and bake for 1 hour or until bird is tender and dust with 1 teaspoon paprika. Serves her right.

CAT ON A HOT
THIN ROOF

Don't Pussyfoot Around

*Alley cats have as noisy an oral history as a city
sanitation truck. On the hottest of summer nights,
the lying, stealing, cheating tom cats scream their
affections and affectations from and through the thin
rooftops. Only a high-speed Checker cab racing up
their alley has a chance to stop this tomfoolery.*

*The old superstition that black cats bring bad luck
to those whose path they cross is meaningless if the
black cat is not able to cross your path!*

There are more ways than one to skin a cat, all pleasur-
able. Clean and remove outer garment from 1 tomcat.
Toss those nasty internal organs and let Tweety Bird
out of stomach. Preheat oven to 300 degrees. In a mixing bowl, combine 2 teaspoons black pepper, 2 teaspoons
salt, 1 teaspoon garlic powder, and 1 teaspoon MSG (the
pearl of the Orient). Rub the now naked and foolish

looking feline with this mixture, then place on a rack inside a roasting pan along with 2 red potatoes, 1 quartered meowie onion, and 2 carrots. Bake for 2 hours. This cat chow serves 1 Big Daddy. Catsup is the traditional sauce for those who sup so.

BUY MORE
BUCK BOOKS!

Buck Peterson, master-guide-to-all-that-is-wild-in-the-outdoors has written a whole slew of books besides this one. In all of them, readers will appreciate the literary equivalent of the chaos theory of creation.

The Original Roadkill Cookbook
Buck Peterson's Complete Guide to Deer Hunting
Buck Peterson's Complete Guide to Fishing
Buck Peterson's Complete Guide to Indoor Life
The Endangered Species Cookbook
The International Roadkill Cookbook
The Complete Waterfouler